GW00494219

BASIC BUTTER CAKE

PREPARATION TIME 30 MINUTES • COOKING TIME 1 HOUR • SERVES 12

250g butter, softened
1 teaspoon vanilla extract
1¼ cups (275g) caster sugar
3 eggs
2¼ cups (335g) self-raising flour
¾ cup (180ml) milk

1 Preheat oven to 180°C/160°C fan-forced. Grease deep 22cm-round or 19cm-square cake pan; line with baking paper.
2 Beat butter, extract and sugar in medium bowl with electric mixer until light and fluffy. Beat in eggs, one at a time. Stir in sifted flour and milk, in two batches.
3 Spread mixture into pan; bake about 1 hour. Stand cake 5 minutes; turn, top-side up, onto wire rack to cool.

MARBLE CAKE

PREPARATION TIME 30 MINUTES (PLUS COOLING TIME) • COOKING TIME 1 HOUR • SERVES 12

----

1 quantity basic butter cake mixture
   (see recipe, above)
pink food colouring
2 tablespoons cocoa powder
2 tablespoons milk, extra
BUTTER FROSTING
90g butter, softened
1 cup (160g) icing sugar
1 tablespoon milk

1 Follow steps 1 and 2 in *basic butter cake* recipe, above.
2 Divide mixture among three bowls; tint one mixture pink. Blend sifted cocoa with extra milk in cup; stir into second mixture. Drop alternate spoonfuls of mixtures into pan.
3 Pull a skewer backwards and forwards through cake mixture.
4 Bake cake about 1 hour. Stand cake 5 minutes; turn, top-side up, onto wire rack to cool. Top with butter frosting.
BUTTER FROSTING Beat butter in small bowl with electric mixer until light and fluffy; beat in sifted icing sugar and milk, in two batches. Tint frosting pink with colouring.

PATTY CAKES WITH GLACE ICING

PREPARATION TIME 15 MINUTES (PLUS COOLING TIME) • COOKING TIME 25 MINUTES • MAKES 24

125g butter, softened
1 teaspoon vanilla extract
⅔ cup (150g) caster sugar
3 eggs
1½ cups (225g) self-raising flour
¼ cup (60ml) milk
GLACE ICING
1½ cups (240g) icing sugar
1 teaspoon butter
2 tablespoons milk, approximately

1 Preheat oven to 180°C/160°C fan-forced. Line two deep 12-hole patty pans with paper cases.
2 Combine butter, extract, sugar, eggs, flour and milk in medium bowl; beat on low speed with electric mixer until ingredients are combined. Increase speed to medium; beat about 3 minutes or until mixture is smooth and paler in colour.
3 Drop slightly rounded tablespoons of mixture into paper cases. Bake about 20 minutes. Turn cakes, top-side up, onto wire racks to cool. Top with glace icing.
GLACE ICING Sift icing sugar into small heatproof bowl; stir in butter and enough milk to give a firm paste. Set bowl over small saucepan of simmering water; stir until icing is spreadable.

marble cake

basic butter cake

patty cakes with glace icing

HOW TO KEEP Butter cakes can be stored, at room temperature, in an airtight container for 2 days, or can be frozen for 2 months.

ECONOMICAL BOILED FRUIT CAKE

PREPARATION TIME 15 MINUTES (PLUS COOLING TIME) • COOKING TIME 1 HOUR 30 MINUTES • SERVES 12

2¾ cups (500g) mixed dried fruit
½ cup (125ml) water
1 cup (220g) firmly packed
   brown sugar
125g butter, chopped
1 teaspoon mixed spice
½ teaspoon bicarbonate of soda
½ cup (125ml) sweet sherry
1 egg
1 cup (150g) plain flour
1 cup (150g) self-raising flour
⅓ cup (55g) blanched almonds
2 tablespoons sweet sherry, extra

1 Combine fruit, the water, sugar, butter, spice and soda in large saucepan. Stir over low heat, without boiling, until sugar dissolves and butter melts; bring to a boil. Reduce heat; simmer, covered, 5 minutes. Remove from heat; stir in sherry. Cool to room temperature.

2 Preheat oven to 160°C/140°C fan-forced. Grease deep 20cm-round cake pan; line base and side with two layers of baking paper, extending paper 5cm above side.

3 Stir egg and sifted flours into fruit mixture. Spread mixture into pan; decorate with almonds. Bake about 1½ hours. Brush top of hot cake with extra sherry. Cover cake with foil, cool in pan.

HOW TO KEEP Fruit cake can be stored in an airtight container for up to 1 month.

CHOCOLATE CAKE

PREPARATION TIME 10 MINUTES (PLUS COOLING TIME) • COOKING TIME 1 HOUR • SERVES 20

125g butter, softened
1 teaspoon vanilla extract
1¼ cups (275g) caster sugar
2 eggs
1⅓ cups (200g) self-raising flour
½ cup (50g) cocoa powder
⅔ cup (160ml) water

CHOCOLATE ICING
90g dark eating chocolate,
   chopped coarsely
30g butter
1 cup (160g) icing sugar
2 tablespoons hot water

1 Preheat oven to 180°C/160°C fan-forced. Grease deep 20cm-round cake pan; line with baking paper.

2 Beat butter, extract, sugar, eggs, sifted flour and cocoa, and the water in large bowl with electric mixer on low speed until ingredients are combined. Increase speed to medium; beat about 3 minutes or until mixture is smooth and paler in colour.

3 Spread mixture into pan; bake about 1 hour. Stand cake 5 minutes; turn, top-side up, onto wire rack to cool.

4 Meanwhile, make chocolate icing. Spread cake with icing.

CHOCOLATE ICING Melt chocolate and butter in small heatproof bowl over small saucepan of simmering water; gradually stir in sifted icing sugar and the hot water, stirring until icing is spreadable.

HOW TO KEEP Chocolate cake can be stored in an airtight container for up to 3 days.

COCONUT CAKE

125g butter, softened
½ teaspoon coconut essence
1 cup (220g) caster sugar
2 eggs
½ cup (40g) desiccated coconut
1½ cups (225g) self-raising flour
1¼ cups (300g) sour cream
⅓ cup (80ml) milk

COCONUT ICE FROSTING

2 cups (320g) icing sugar
1⅓ cups (100g) desiccated coconut
2 egg whites, beaten lightly
pink food colouring

1 Preheat oven to 180°C/160°C fan-forced. Grease deep 23cm-square cake pan; line with baking paper.

2 Beat butter, essence and sugar in small bowl with electric mixer until light and fluffy. Beat in eggs, one at a time. Transfer mixture to large bowl; stir in coconut, sifted flour, sour cream and milk, in two batches.

3 Spread mixture into pan; bake about 40 minutes. Stand cake 5 minutes; turn, top-side up, onto wire rack to cool.

4 Meanwhile, make coconut ice frosting. Drop alternate spoonfuls of white and pink frosting onto cake; marble over top of cake.

COCONUT ICE FROSTING Sift icing sugar into medium bowl; stir in coconut and egg white. Place half the mixture in small bowl; tint with pink colouring.

HOW TO KEEP Coconut cake can be stored in an airtight container for up to 1 week.

DARK CHOCOLATE MUD CAKE

PREPARATION TIME 20 MINUTES (PLUS COOLING TIME) • COOKING TIME 2 HOURS 40 MINUTES • SERVES 16

675g dark eating chocolate, chopped
400g unsalted butter, chopped
1½ tablespoons instant coffee granules
1¼ cups (310ml) water
1¼ cups (275g) firmly packed
   brown sugar
1¾ cups (260g) plain flour
½ cup (75g) self-raising flour
4 eggs
⅓ cup (80ml) coffee-flavoured liqueur
DARK CHOCOLATE GANACHE
½ cup (125ml) cream
400g dark eating chocolate, chopped

1 Preheat oven to 160°C/140°C fan-forced. Grease deep 19cm-square cake pan; line with baking paper.
2 Combine chocolate, butter, coffee, the water and sugar in large saucepan; stir over low heat until smooth. Cool 15 minutes.
3 Whisk in sifted flours, eggs and liqueur. Pour mixture into pan; bake about 2½ hours. Cool cake in pan.
4 Meanwhile, make dark chocolate ganache.
5 Turn cake, top-side up, onto plate; spread with ganache. Top with raspberries, if desired.
DARK CHOCOLATE GANACHE Bring cream to a boil in small saucepan; remove from heat, add chocolate, stir until smooth. Refrigerate, stirring occasionally, about 30 minutes or until spreadable.

CARAMEL MUD CAKE

PREPARATION TIME 20 MINUTES (PLUS COOLING TIME) • COOKING TIME 1 HOUR 40 MINUTES • SERVES 12

180g white eating chocolate, chopped
185g unsalted butter, chopped
1 cup (220g) firmly packed
   brown sugar
⅓ cup (80ml) golden syrup
1 cup (250ml) milk
1½ cups (225g) plain flour
½ cup (75g) self-raising flour
2 eggs
WHITE CHOCOLATE GANACHE
½ cup (125ml) cream
360g white eating chocolate, chopped

1 Preheat oven to 160°C/140°C fan-forced. Grease deep 22cm-round cake pan; line with baking paper.
2 Combine chocolate, butter, sugar, syrup and milk in large saucepan; stir over low heat until smooth. Cool 15 minutes.
3 Whisk in sifted flours and eggs. Pour mixture into pan; bake about 1½ hours. Cool cake in pan.
4 Meanwhile, make white chocolate ganache.
5 Turn cake, top-side up, onto plate; spread with ganache.
WHITE CHOCOLATE GANACHE Bring cream to a boil in small saucepan, remove from heat; add chocolate, stir until smooth. Refrigerate, stirring occasionally, about 30 minutes or until spreadable.

WHITE MUD CAKE

PREPARATION TIME 20 MINUTES (PLUS COOLING TIME) • COOKING TIME 2 HOURS 10 MINUTES • SERVES 12

180g white chocolate, chopped
350g unsalted butter, chopped
2⅔ cups (590g) caster sugar
1½ cups (375ml) milk
2 cups (300g) plain flour
⅔ cup (100g) self-raising flour
1 teaspoon vanilla extract
3 eggs
1 quantity white chocolate ganache

1 Preheat oven to 160°C/140°C fan-forced. Grease deep 22cm-round cake pan; line with baking paper.
2 Combine chocolate, butter, sugar and milk in large saucepan; stir over low heat until smooth. Pour mixture into large bowl; cool 15 minutes.
3 Whisk in sifted flours, extract and eggs. Pour mixture into pan; bake about 2 hours. Cool cake in pan.
4 Turn cake, top-side up, onto plate; spread with ganache (see recipe, above).

dark chocolate mud cake

caramel mud cake

white mud cake

Mud cakes can be
stored, refrigerated, in an airtight container
for 1 week, or can be frozen for 2 months.

APPLE STREUSEL CAKE

PREPARATION TIME 25 MINUTES (PLUS FREEZING TIME) • COOKING TIME 50 MINUTES • SERVES 16

200g butter, softened
2 teaspoons finely grated lemon rind
⅔ cup (150g) caster sugar
3 eggs
1 cup (150g) self-raising flour
½ cup (75g) plain flour
⅓ cup (80ml) milk
5 medium apples (750g)
25g butter, extra
⅓ cup (75g) firmly packed brown sugar

STREUSEL
½ cup (75g) plain flour
¼ cup (35g) self-raising flour
⅓ cup (75g) firmly packed brown sugar
½ teaspoon ground cinnamon
80g butter, chopped finely

1   Preheat oven to 180°C/160°C fan-forced. Grease deep 23cm-round cake pan; line with baking paper.
2   Make streusel.
3   Beat butter, rind and caster sugar in small bowl with electric mixer until light and fluffy. Beat in eggs, one at a time. Transfer to large bowl; stir in sifted flours and milk, in two batches. Spread mixture into pan; bake 25 minutes.
4   Meanwhile, peel, core and quarter apples; slice thinly. Melt extra butter in large frying pan; cook apple, stirring, about 5 minutes or until browned lightly. Add brown sugar; cook, stirring, about 5 minutes or until mixture thickens slightly. Set aside.
5   Remove cake from oven. Working quickly, top cake with apple mixture; coarsely grate streusel over apple. Return to oven; bake about 25 minutes. Stand cake 10 minutes; turn, top-side up, onto wire rack to cool. Serve cake warm or cold.
STREUSEL   Process flours, sugar and cinnamon until combined. Add butter; process until ingredients just come together. Wrap in plastic wrap; freeze about 1 hour or until firm.
HOW TO KEEP   Apple streusel cake can be stored in an airtight container for up to 4 days.

LAMINGTONS

PREPARATION TIME 25 MINUTES • COOKING TIME 35 MINUTES • MAKES 16

6 eggs
⅔ cup (150g) caster sugar
⅓ cup (50g) cornflour
½ cup (75g) plain flour
⅓ cup (50g) self-raising flour
2 cups (160g) desiccated coconut
ICING
4 cups (640g) icing sugar
½ cup (50g) cocoa powder
15g butter, melted
1 cup (250ml) milk

1 Preheat oven to 180°C/160°C fan-forced. Grease 20cm x 30cm lamington pan; line with baking paper, extending paper 5cm over long sides.
2 Beat eggs in large bowl with electric mixer about 10 minutes or until thick and creamy; gradually beat in sugar, dissolving between additions. Fold in triple-sifted flours.
3 Spread mixture into pan; bake about 35 minutes. Turn cake immediately onto a baking-paper-covered wire rack to cool.
4 Meanwhile, make icing. Cut cake into 16 pieces; dip each square in icing, drain off excess. Toss squares in coconut. Place lamingtons onto wire rack to set.
ICING Sift icing sugar and cocoa into medium heatproof bowl; stir in butter and milk. Set bowl over medium saucepan of simmering water; stir until icing is of a coating consistency.
HOW TO KEEP Unfilled lamingtons can be stored in an airtight container for up to 3 days.

VARIATIONS

PINK JELLY CAKES Make 80g packet of strawberry jelly as per packet instructions; refrigerate until set to consistency of unbeaten egg white. Dip cake squares into jelly then desiccated coconut. Beat 300ml thickened cream until firm peaks form. Halve cakes horizontally; sandwich cakes with whipped cream.
MOCHA LAMINGTONS Add 1 tablespoon cocoa powder to dry ingredients for cake; fold into egg mixture. Combine 1 tablespoon instant coffee granules with 1 tablespoon boiling water; fold into cake mixture then follow instructions from step 3 of lamington recipe. Beat 300ml thickened cream with 2 tablespoons coffee-flavoured liqueur until firm peaks form. Once icing has set, halve lamingtons horizontally then sandwich cakes with whipped cream.

LEMON SYRUP CAKE

PREPARATION TIME 15 MINUTES • COOKING TIME 50 MINUTES • SERVES 12

250g butter, softened
1 tablespoon finely grated lemon rind
1 cup (220g) caster sugar
3 eggs
1 cup (250ml) buttermilk
⅓ cup (80ml) lemon juice
2 cups (300g) self-raising flour

LEMON SYRUP
⅓ cup (80ml) lemon juice
¼ cup (60ml) water
¾ cup (165g) caster sugar

1 Preheat oven to 180°C/160°C fan-forced. Grease 24cm baba pan or deep 22cm-round cake pan.

2 Beat butter, rind and sugar in small bowl with electric mixer until light and fluffy. Beat in eggs, one at a time. Transfer to large bowl; fold in buttermilk, lemon juice and sifted flour, in two batches.

3 Spread mixture into pan; bake about 50 minutes if using baba pan or bake about 1 hour if using round pan. Cover cake with foil if browning too quickly. Stand cake 5 minutes; turn onto wire rack set over tray.

4 Meanwhile, make lemon syrup. Pour hot syrup over hot cake; serve warm.

LEMON SYRUP Combine ingredients in small saucepan; stir over heat, without boiling, until sugar dissolves. Simmer, uncovered, without stirring, 5 minutes.

HOW TO KEEP Lemon syrup cake can be stored in an airtight container for up to 2 days.

WENDY'S SPONGE CAKE

PREPARATION TIME 20 MINUTES • COOKING TIME 20 MINUTES • SERVES 10

- -

4 eggs
¾ cup (165g) caster sugar
⅔ cup (100g) wheaten cornflour
¼ cup (30g) custard powder
1 teaspoon cream of tartar
½ teaspoon bicarbonate of soda
⅓ cup (110g) apricot jam
300ml thickened cream, whipped

1 Preheat oven to 180°C/160°C fan-forced. Grease and flour two deep 22cm-round cake pans.
2 Beat eggs and sugar in small bowl with electric mixer until thick, creamy and sugar dissolved; transfer to large bowl.
3 Fold in triple-sifted dry ingredients. Divide mixture between pans; bake about 20 minutes. Turn sponges, top-side up, onto baking-paper-lined wire rack to cool.
4 Sandwich sponges with jam and cream.

SPONGE ROLL WITH JAM AND CREAM

PREPARATION TIME 25 MINUTES (PLUS REFRIGERATION TIME) • COOKING TIME 12 MINUTES • SERVES 10

- -

3 eggs
⅔ cup (150g) caster sugar
½ cup (75g) wheaten cornflour
2 tablespoons custard powder
¾ teaspoon cream of tartar
½ teaspoon bicarbonate of soda
⅓ cup (110g) raspberry jam
¾ cup (180ml) thickened cream, whipped

1 Preheat oven to 180°C/160°C fan-forced. Grease 25cm x 30cm swiss roll pan; line base with baking paper, extending paper 5cm over long sides.
2 Beat eggs and ½ cup of the caster sugar in small bowl with electric mixer until thick, creamy and sugar dissolved.
3 Fold in triple-sifted dry ingredients. Spread mixture into pan; bake about 12 minutes.
4 Meanwhile, place piece of baking paper cut the same size as pan on bench; sprinkle with remaining caster sugar. Turn sponge onto paper; peel lining paper away. Cool; trim all sides of sponge.
5 Spread sponge with jam then cream. Using paper as a guide, roll sponge from short side. Cover with plastic wrap; refrigerate 30 minutes.

GINGER FLUFF ROLL

PREPARATION TIME 25 MINUTES (PLUS REFRIGERATION TIME) • COOKING TIME 12 MINUTES • SERVES 10

- -

3 eggs
⅔ cup (150g) caster sugar
⅔ cup (100g) wheaten cornflour
1 teaspoon cream of tartar
½ teaspoon bicarbonate of soda
1 teaspoon cocoa powder
2 teaspoons ground ginger
½ teaspoon ground cinnamon
¾ cup (180ml) thickened cream
2 tablespoons golden syrup
1 teaspoon ground ginger, extra

1 Preheat oven to 180°C/160°C fan-forced. Grease 25cm x 30cm swiss roll pan; line base with baking paper, extending paper 5cm over long sides.
2 Beat eggs and ½ cup of the sugar in small bowl with electric mixer until thick, creamy and sugar dissolved.
3 Fold in triple-sifted dry ingredients. Spread sponge mixture into pan; bake about 12 minutes.
4 Meanwhile, place piece of baking paper cut the same size as pan on bench; sprinkle with remaining caster sugar. Turn sponge onto paper; peel lining paper away. Cool; trim all sides of sponge.
5 Make ginger cream by beating cream, syrup and extra ginger in small bowl with electric mixer until firm peaks form. Spread sponge with cream. Using paper as a guide, roll sponge from long side. Cover with plastic wrap; refrigerate 30 minutes.

sponge roll with jam and cream

wendy's sponge cake

ginger fluff roll

HOW TO KEEP Unfilled sponges can be frozen for up to 2 months. Filled sponges and rolls are best eaten on the day they are made.

BERRY MUFFINS

PREPARATION TIME 10 MINUTES • COOKING TIME 20 MINUTES • MAKES 12

2½ cups (375g) self-raising flour
90g cold butter, chopped
1 cup (220g) caster sugar
1¼ cups (310ml) buttermilk
1 egg, beaten lightly
200g fresh or frozen mixed berries

1 Preheat oven to 180°C/160°C fan-forced. Grease 12-hole (⅓-cup/80ml) muffin pan.

2 Sift flour into large bowl; rub in butter. Stir in sugar, buttermilk and egg. Do not over-mix; mixture should be lumpy. Add berries; stir through gently.

3 Spoon mixture into pan holes; bake about 20 minutes. Stand muffins 5 minutes; turn, top-side up, onto wire rack to cool.

HOW TO KEEP Muffins can be stored in an airtight container for up to 2 days.

VARIATIONS

LEMON POPPY SEED Omit berries. Add 2 teaspoons lemon rind and 2 tablespoons poppy seeds with the sugar.

DATE AND ORANGE Omit berries. Substitute self-raising flour with 1 cup wholemeal self-raising flour and 1½ cups white self-raising flour. Add 1½ cups seeded, chopped dried dates and 2 teaspoons finely grated orange rind with the sugar.

CHOC CHIP AND WALNUT Omit mixed berries. Add ¾ cup dark Choc Bits and 1 cup coarsely chopped walnuts with the sugar.

ORANGE CAKE

150g butter, softened
1 tablespoon finely grated orange rind
⅔ cup (150g) caster sugar
3 eggs
1½ cups (225g) self-raising flour
¼ cup (60ml) milk
¾ cup (120g) icing sugar
1½ tablespoons orange juice

1 Preheat oven to 180°C/160°C fan-forced. Grease deep 20cm-round cake pan.

2 Beat butter, rind, caster sugar, eggs, flour and milk in medium bowl with electric mixer at low speed until just combined. Increase speed to medium, beat about 3 minutes or until mixture is smooth.

3 Spread mixture into pan; bake about 40 minutes. Stand cake 5 minutes; turn, top-side up, onto wire rack to cool.

4 Combine sifted icing sugar and juice in small bowl; spread over cake.

HOW TO KEEP Orange cake can be stored in an airtight container for up to 4 days.

MADEIRA CAKE

PREPARATION TIME 15 MINUTES • COOKING TIME 1 HOUR • SERVES 12

180g butter, softened
2 teaspoons finely grated lemon rind
⅔ cup (150g) caster sugar
3 eggs
¾ cup (110g) plain flour
¾ cup (110g) self-raising flour
⅓ cup (55g) mixed peel
¼ cup (35g) slivered almonds

1 Preheat oven to 160°C/140°C fan-forced. Grease deep 20cm-round cake pan; line base with paper.
2 Beat butter, rind and sugar in small bowl with electric mixer until light and fluffy; beat in eggs, one at a time. Transfer mixture to large bowl, stir in sifted flours.
3 Spread mixture into pan; bake 20 minutes. Remove cake from oven; sprinkle with peel and nuts. Return to oven; bake about 40 minutes. Stand cake 5 minutes; turn, top-side up, onto wire rack to cool.
HOW TO KEEP Madeira cake can be stored in an airtight container for up to 4 days.

ROCK CAKES

PREPARATION TIME 15 MINUTES • COOKING TIME 15 MINUTES • MAKES 18

2 cups (300g) self-raising flour
¼ teaspoon ground cinnamon
⅓ cup (75g) caster sugar
90g butter, chopped
1 cup (160g) sultanas
1 egg, beaten lightly
½ cup (125ml) milk
1 tablespoon caster sugar, extra

1 Preheat oven to 200°C/180°C fan-forced. Grease oven trays.
2 Sift flour, cinnamon and sugar into medium bowl; rub in butter. Stir in sultanas, egg and milk. Do not over mix.
3 Drop rounded tablespoons of mixture about 5cm apart onto trays; sprinkle with extra sugar. Bake about 15 minutes; cool on trays.

HOW TO KEEP Rock cakes can be stored in an airtight container for up to 2 days.

VARIATIONS

CRAISIN AND FIG Substitute caster sugar with ⅓ cup firmly packed brown sugar. Omit sultanas; stir 1 cup coarsely chopped dried figs and ¼ cup craisins into mixture before egg and milk are added.

PINEAPPLE, LIME AND COCONUT Omit sultanas; stir 1 cup coarsely chopped dried pineapple, ¼ cup toasted flaked coconut and 1 teaspoon finely grated lime rind into mixture before egg and milk are added.

BANANA CAKE WITH PASSIONFRUIT ICING

PREPARATION TIME 35 MINUTES (PLUS COOLING TIME) • COOKING TIME 50 MINUTES • SERVES 10

You need approximately two large overripe bananas (460g) for this recipe as well as two large passionfruits.

125g butter, softened
¾ cup (165g) firmly packed
   brown sugar
2 eggs
1½ cups (225g) self-raising flour
½ teaspoon bicarbonate of soda
1 teaspoon mixed spice
1 cup mashed banana
½ cup (120g) sour cream
¼ cup (60ml) milk

PASSIONFRUIT ICING

1½ cups (240g) icing sugar
1 teaspoon soft butter
2 tablespoons passionfruit pulp,
   approximately

1 Preheat oven to 180°C/160°C. Grease 15cm x 25cm loaf pan; line base with baking paper.
2 Beat butter and sugar in small bowl with electric mixer until light and fluffy. Beat in eggs, one at a time. Transfer to large bowl; stir in sifted dry ingredients, banana, sour cream and milk.
3 Spread mixture into pan; bake about 50 minutes. Stand cake 5 minutes; turn, top-side up, onto wire rack to cool.
4 Meanwhile, make passionfruit icing. Spread cake with icing.

PASSIONFRUIT ICING Combine ingredients in medium bowl.

HOW TO KEEP Banana cake can be stored in an airtight container for up to 4 days.

DESSERTS

ALMOND PEAR FLAN

PREPARATION TIME 30 MINUTES (PLUS REFRIGERATION TIME) • COOKING TIME 45 MINUTES • SERVES 10

1¼ cups (185g) plain flour
90g butter
¼ cup (55g) caster sugar
2 egg yolks
3 firm ripe medium pears (690g),
    peeled, cored, quartered
2 tablespoons apricot jam,
    warmed, strained

ALMOND FILLING

125g butter
⅓ cup (75g) caster sugar
2 eggs
1 cup (120g) almond meal
1 tablespoon plain flour

1   Blend or process flour, butter, sugar and egg yolks until just combined. Knead on floured surface until smooth, cover; refrigerate 30 minutes.

2   Meanwhile, make almond filling.

3   Preheat oven to 180°C/160°C fan-forced. Grease 23cm-round loose-based flan tin.

4   Roll dough between sheets of baking paper; press dough evenly into base and side of tin. Spread filling into pastry case; arrange pears over filling. Bake about 45 minutes. Brush flan with jam.

ALMOND FILLING   Beat butter and sugar in small bowl with electric mixer until just combined. Add eggs, one at a time; fold in meal and flour.

TIP   Pears can be replaced with apples, peaches, plums, apricots or blueberries.

HOW TO KEEP   Flan can be stored in an airtight container for up to 2 days.

GOLDEN SYRUP DUMPLINGS

1¼ cups (185g) self-raising flour
30g butter
⅓ cup (115g) golden syrup
⅓ cup (80ml) milk
SAUCE
30g butter
¾ cup (165g) firmly packed
  brown sugar
½ cup (175g) golden syrup
1⅔ cups (410ml) water

1 Sift flour into medium bowl; rub in butter. Gradually stir in golden syrup and milk.

2 Make sauce.

3 Drop rounded tablespoonfuls of mixture into simmering sauce; simmer, covered, about 20 minutes. Serve dumplings with sauce.

SAUCE Combine ingredients in medium saucepan; stir over heat, without boiling, until sugar dissolves. Bring to a boil, without stirring. Reduce heat; simmer, uncovered, 5 minutes.

APPLE PIE

PREPARATION TIME 45 MINUTES (PLUS REFRIGERATION TIME) • COOKING TIME 1 HOUR 10 MINUTES • SERVES 8

10 medium Granny Smith apples
(1.5kg), peeled, cored, sliced thickly
½ cup (125ml) water
¼ cup (55g) caster sugar
1 teaspoon finely grated lemon rind
¼ teaspoon ground cinnamon
1 tablespoon caster sugar, extra

PASTRY
1 cup (150g) plain flour
½ cup (75g) self-raising flour
¼ cup (35g) cornflour
¼ cup (30g) custard powder
1 tablespoon caster sugar
100g cold butter, chopped
1 egg, separated
¼ cup (60ml) cold water

1 Make pastry.
2 Place apple with the water in large saucepan; bring to a boil. Reduce heat; simmer, covered, about 10 minutes or until apples soften. Drain; stir in sugar, rind and cinnamon. Cool.
3 Preheat oven to 220°C/200°C fan-forced. Grease deep 25cm pie dish.
4 Divide pastry in half. Roll one half between sheets of baking paper until large enough to line dish. Spoon apple mixture into dish; brush pastry edge with egg white.
5 Roll remaining pastry large enough to cover filling. Press edges together. Brush pastry with egg white; sprinkle with extra sugar. Bake 20 minutes. Reduce oven temperature to 180°C/160°C fan-forced; bake a further 25 minutes.
PASTRY Process dry ingredients and butter until crumbly. Add egg yolk and the water; process until combined. Knead on floured surface until smooth. Cover; refrigerate 30 minutes.

APPLE DATE AND ORANGE PIE

PREPARATION TIME 45 MINUTES (PLUS REFRIGERATION TIME) • COOKING TIME 1 HOUR 10 MINUTES • SERVES 8

1 quantity pastry (see *apple pie* recipe)
8 medium Granny Smith apples
(1.2kg), peeled, cored, sliced thickly
½ cup (125ml) water
1½ cups (210g) coarsely chopped
dried dates
¼ cup (55g) caster sugar
2 teaspoons finely grated orange rind
1 tablespoon demerara sugar

1 Stew apple with the water, as per step 2 of *apple pie* recipe; add dates after 5 minutes. Drain; stir in caster sugar and rind. Cool.
2 Preheat oven to 220°C/200°C fan-forced. Grease deep 25cm pie dish.
3 Divide pastry in half. Roll one half between sheets of baking paper until large enough to line dish. Spoon apple mixture into dish; brush pastry edges with egg white.
4 Roll remaining pastry large enough to cover filling. Press edges together. Brush pastry with egg white; sprinkle with demerara sugar. Bake 20 minutes. Reduce oven temperature to 180°C/160°C fan-forced; bake a further 25 minutes.

APRICOT AND ALMOND APPLE PIE

PREPARATION TIME 45 MINUTES (PLUS REFRIGERATION TIME) • COOKING TIME 1 HOUR 10 MINUTES • SERVES 8

1 quantity pastry (see *apple pie* recipe)
10 medium Granny Smith apples
(1.5kg), peeled, cored, sliced thickly
½ cup (125ml) water
1 tablespoon caster sugar
⅔ cup (220g) apricot jam
1 teaspoon finely grated lemon rind
¼ cup (20g) flaked almonds

1 Stew apple with the water, as per step 2 of *apple pie* recipe. Drain; stir in sugar, jam and rind. Cool.
2 Preheat oven to 220°C/200°C fan-forced. Grease deep 25cm pie dish.
3 Divide pastry in half. Roll one half between sheets of baking paper until large enough to line dish. Spoon apple mixture into dish; brush pastry edge with egg white.
4 Roll remaining pastry large enough to cover filling. Press edges together. Brush pastry with egg white; sprinkle with almonds. Bake 20 minutes. Reduce oven temperature to 180°C/160°C fan-forced; bake a further 25 minutes.

apple date and orange pie

apricot and almond apple pie

apple pie

HOW TO KEEP Pies can be stored, refrigerated, in an airtight container for up to 1 day.

BAKED CUSTARD

PREPARATION TIME 5 MINUTES • COOKING TIME 45 MINUTES • SERVES 6

6 eggs
1 teaspoon vanilla extract
⅓ cup (75g) caster sugar
1 litre (4 cups) hot milk
¼ teaspoon ground nutmeg

1 Preheat oven to 160°C/140°C fan-forced. Grease shallow 1.5-litre (6-cup) ovenproof dish.

2 Whisk eggs, extract and sugar in large bowl; gradually whisk in hot milk. Pour custard mixture into dish; sprinkle with nutmeg.

3 Place dish in larger baking dish; add enough boiling water to come halfway up sides of dish. Bake, uncovered, about 45 minutes. Remove custard from large dish; stand 5 minutes before serving.

VARIATIONS

CITRUS Stir ½ teaspoon each of finely grated orange, lime and lemon rind into hot milk mixture; omit nutmeg.

CHOCOLATE Whisk ⅓ cup cocoa powder and ⅓ cup dark Choc Bits with eggs, extract and sugar; omit nutmeg.

COCONUT AND CARDAMOM Omit hot milk; bring 2⅓ cups milk, 400ml can coconut milk, 3 bruised cardamom pods and 5cm strip lime rind to a boil. Remove from heat, stand 10 minutes. Strain; discard solids. Whisk milk mixture into egg mixture.

CHOCOLATE SOUFFLÉ

PREPARATION TIME 15 MINUTES • COOKING TIME 20 MINUTES • SERVES 4

⅓ cup (75g) caster sugar
50g butter
1 tablespoon plain flour
200g dark eating chocolate, melted
2 egg yolks
4 egg whites

1 Preheat oven to 180°C/160°C fan-forced. Grease four ¾-cup (180ml) soufflé dishes. Sprinkle inside of dishes with a little of the sugar; shake away excess. Place dishes on oven tray.

2 Melt butter in small saucepan, add flour; cook, stirring, about 2 minutes or until mixture thickens and bubbles. Remove from heat; stir in chocolate and egg yolks. Transfer to large bowl.

3 Beat egg whites in small bowl with electric mixer until soft peaks form. Gradually add remaining sugar, beating until sugar dissolves. Fold egg white mixture into chocolate mixture, in two batches.

4 Divide soufflé mixture among dishes; bake 15 minutes. Dust with cocoa powder, if desired.

It is believed that this dessert, originally called banoffi pie (the sound of the made-up word coming from a mix of banana and toffee), was developed by an East Sussex restaurateur in 1971.

BANOFFEE PIE

PREPARATION TIME 45 MINUTES (PLUS REFRIGERATION TIME) • COOKING TIME 35 MINUTES • SERVES 8

395g can sweetened condensed milk
75g butter, chopped
½ cup (110g) firmly packed
   brown sugar
2 tablespoons golden syrup
2 large bananas (460g), sliced thinly
300ml thickened cream, whipped

PASTRY

1½ cups (225g) plain flour
1 tablespoon icing sugar
140g cold butter, chopped
1 egg yolk
2 tablespoons cold water

1 Make pastry.

2 Grease 24cm-round loose-based fluted flan tin. Roll dough between sheets of baking paper until large enough to line tin. Ease dough into tin; press into base and side. Trim edge; prick base all over with fork. Cover; refrigerate 30 minutes.

3 Preheat oven to 200°C/180°C fan-forced.

4 Place tin on oven tray; cover dough with baking paper, fill with dried beans or rice. Bake 10 minutes; remove paper and beans carefully from pie shell. Bake a further 10 minutes; cool.

5 Meanwhile, combine condensed milk, butter, sugar and syrup in medium saucepan; cook over medium heat, stirring, about 10 minutes or until mixture is caramel-coloured. Stand 5 minutes; pour into pie shell, cool.

6 Top caramel with banana; top with whipped cream.

PASTRY Process flour, sugar and butter until crumbly; add egg yolk and water, process until ingredients come together. Knead dough on floured surface until smooth. Wrap in plastic; refrigerate 30 minutes.

BREAD AND BUTTER PUDDING
PREPARATION TIME 20 MINUTES • COOKING TIME 50 MINUTES • SERVES 6

6 slices white bread (270g)
40g butter, softened
½ cup (80g) sultanas
¼ teaspoon ground nutmeg
CUSTARD
1½ cups (375ml) milk
2 cups (500ml) cream
⅓ cup (75g) caster sugar
½ teaspoon vanilla extract
4 eggs

1 Preheat oven to 160°C/140°C fan-forced.
2 Make custard.
3 Grease shallow 2-litre (8-cup) ovenproof dish. Trim crusts from bread. Spread each slice with butter; cut into 4 triangles. Layer bread, overlapping, in dish; sprinkle with sultanas. Pour custard over bread; sprinkle with nutmeg.
4 Place dish in large baking dish; add enough boiling water to come halfway up sides of dish. Bake about 45 minutes or until pudding sets. Remove pudding from baking dish; stand 5 minutes before serving.
CUSTARD Combine milk, cream, sugar and extract in medium saucepan; bring to a boil. Whisk eggs in large bowl; whisking constantly, gradually add hot milk mixture to egg mixture.

CHOCOLATE PECAN PUDDING
PREPARATION TIME 20 MINUTES • COOKING TIME 50 MINUTES • SERVES 6

1 quantity custard (see *bread and butter pudding* recipe, above)
200g ciabatta, sliced thickly
100g dark eating chocolate, chopped coarsely
⅓ cup (40g) coarsely chopped roasted pecans

1 Preheat oven to 160°C/140°C fan-forced.
2 Grease shallow 2-litre (8-cup) ovenproof dish. Layer bread, chocolate and nuts, overlapping slices slightly, in dish. Pour custard over bread.
3 Place dish in large baking dish; add enough boiling water to come halfway up sides of dish. Bake about 45 minutes or until pudding sets. Remove pudding from baking dish; stand 5 minutes before serving.

FRUIT MINCE AND BRIOCHE PUDDING
PREPARATION TIME 20 MINUTES • COOKING TIME 50 MINUTES • SERVES 6

1 quantity custard (see *bread and butter pudding* recipe, above)
475g jar fruit mince
2 tablespoons brandy
300g brioche, sliced thickly
1 tablespoon demerara sugar

1 Preheat oven to 160°C/140°C fan-forced.
2 Combine fruit mince and brandy in small bowl.
3 Grease shallow 2-litre (8-cup) ovenproof dish. Layer bread and half the fruit mixture, overlapping bread slightly, in dish. Dollop spoonfuls of remaining fruit mixture over bread. Pour custard over bread; sprinkle with sugar.
4 Place dish in large baking dish; add enough boiling water to come halfway up sides of dish. Bake about 45 minutes or until pudding sets. Remove pudding from baking dish; stand 5 minutes before serving.

chocolate pecan pudding

bread and butter pudding

fruit mince and brioche pudding

HOW TO KEEP Puddings can
be stored, refrigerated, in an airtight
container for up to 2 days.

CHOCOLATE MOUSSE

PREPARATION TIME 20 MINUTES (PLUS COOLING AND REFRIGERATION TIME)

COOKING TIME 5 MINUTES • SERVES 6

200g dark eating chocolate,
  chopped coarsely
30g unsalted butter
3 eggs, separated
300ml thickened cream, whipped

1   Melt chocolate in medium heatproof bowl over medium saucepan of simmering water. Remove from heat; add butter, stir until smooth. Stir in egg yolks. Transfer mixture to large bowl, cover; cool.

2   Beat egg whites in small bowl with electric mixer until soft peaks form. Fold egg whites and cream into chocolate mixture, in two batches.

3   Divide mousse among serving dishes; refrigerate 3 hours or overnight. Serve with extra whipped cream, chocolate curls and fresh raspberries, if desired.

HOW TO KEEP   Store mousse, covered, in refrigerator for up to 2 days.

CARAMELISED BANANAS

PREPARATION TIME 10 MINUTES • COOKING TIME 5 MINUTES • SERVES 4

100g butter
⅓ cup (75g) firmly packed
  brown sugar
¾ cup (165g) caster sugar
2 tablespoons water
½ cup (125ml) cream
4 large ripe bananas (920g),
  sliced thickly

1 Heat butter in large frying pan; add sugars and the water. Stir over heat, without boiling, until sugar dissolves; stir in cream. Bring to a boil; add banana, stir gently to coat in caramel.
2 Serve with cream or ice-cream, if desired.

APPLE CRUMBLE

PREPARATION TIME 15 MINUTES • COOKING TIME 35 MINUTES • SERVES 4

5 large apples (1kg)
¼ cup (55g) caster sugar
¼ cup (60ml) water
CRUMBLE
½ cup (75g) self-raising flour
¼ cup (35g) plain flour
½ cup (110g) firmly packed
    brown sugar
100g cold butter, chopped
1 teaspoon ground cinnamon

1 Preheat oven to 180°C/160°C fan-forced. Grease deep
1.5-litre (6-cup) baking dish.
2 Peel, core and quarter apples. Combine apple, sugar and
the water in large saucepan; cook over low heat, covered,
about 10 minutes. Drain; discard liquid.
3 Meanwhile, make crumble.
4 Place apples in dish; sprinkle with crumble. Bake about
25 minutes.
CRUMBLE Blend or process ingredients until combined.

VARIATIONS

NUT CRUMBLE Stir in ⅓ cup roasted slivered almonds and
⅓ cup coarsely chopped roasted hazelnuts to crumble mixture.
MUESLI CRUMBLE Prepare half the amount of basic
crumble mixture; stir in 1 cup toasted muesli.

COLLEGE PUDDING

PREPARATION TIME 15 MINUTES • COOKING TIME 25 MINUTES • SERVES 4

⅓ cup (110g) raspberry jam
1 egg
½ cup (110g) caster sugar
1 cup (150g) self-raising flour
½ cup (125ml) milk
25g butter, melted
1 tablespoon boiling water
1 teaspoon vanilla extract

1 Grease four 1-cup (250ml) metal moulds; divide jam among moulds.

2 Beat egg and sugar in small bowl with electric mixer until thick and creamy. Fold in sifted flour and milk, in two batches; fold in combined butter, the water and extract.

3 Top jam with pudding mixture. Cover each mould with pleated baking paper and foil (to allow puddings to expand as they cook); secure with kitchen string.

4 Place puddings in large saucepan with enough boiling water to come halfway up sides of moulds. Cover pan with tight-fitting lid; boil 25 minutes, replenishing water as necessary to maintain level. Stand puddings 5 minutes before turning onto plate. Serve with cream, if desired.

VARIATION

GOLDEN SYRUP Replace the raspberry jam with ⅓ cup golden syrup.

CHERRIES JUBILEE

PREPARATION TIME 5 MINUTES • COOKING TIME 10 MINUTES • SERVES 4

425g can seeded black cherries
1 tablespoon caster sugar
1 cinnamon stick
2 teaspoons arrowroot
1 tablespoon water
⅓ cup (80ml) brandy

1 Drain cherries, reserve syrup. Combine syrup, sugar and cinnamon in small saucepan; cook, stirring, until mixture boils. Reduce heat; simmer, uncovered, without stirring, 2 minutes. Strain syrup into small heatproof bowl; discard cinnamon.
2 Return syrup to pan; stir in blended arrowroot and the water. Cook, stirring, until mixture boils and thickens slightly. Add cherries; stir until heated through.
3 Heat brandy in small saucepan; stir into cherry mixture. Serve immediately, with thickened cream and macaroons, if desired.

PEACH MELBA

PREPARATION TIME 5 MINUTES (PLUS COOLING TIME) • COOKING TIME 5 MINUTES • SERVES 4

1 litre (4 cups) water
4 medium peaches (600g)
500ml vanilla ice-cream
RASPBERRY SAUCE
200g fresh or thawed
    frozen raspberries
1 tablespoon icing sugar, approximately

1 Place the water in medium saucepan; bring to a boil. Add peaches; simmer, uncovered, 5 minutes. Remove peaches; place in bowl of cold water. When peaches are cold, remove skins. Meanwhile, make raspberry sauce.
2 Serve peach halves topped with ice-cream, sauce and extra raspberries, if desired.
RASPBERRY SAUCE   Push raspberries through fine sieve into small bowl; sweeten pulp with sifted sugar to taste.

STRAWBERRIES ROMANOFF

PREPARATION TIME 10 MINUTES (PLUS REFRIGERATION TIME) • SERVES 4

500g strawberries, halved
1½ tablespoons orange-flavoured
    liqueur
2 teaspoons icing sugar
2 tablespoons icing sugar, extra
½ cup (125ml) thickened cream

1 Combine strawberries, liqueur and icing sugar in large bowl; refrigerate 30 minutes. Drain strawberries over small bowl; reserve liquid. Divide three-quarters of the strawberries among serving dishes.
2 Blend or process remaining strawberries, extra icing sugar and reserved liquid until smooth. Beat cream in small bowl with electric mixer until soft peaks form; fold in strawberry mixture.
3 Top strawberries with strawberry cream.

peach melba

cherries jubilee

strawberries romanoff

HOW TO KEEP All
three fruit desserts are best
made just before serving.

Perhaps the most famous "pancakes" in the world, crêpes suzette have a romantic history that evokes high society and midnight suppers. Restaurants can flame them at the table in a chafing dish for a spectacular finale, but we recommend you ignite them with a long match in the kitchen, with your exhaust fan off, then carry the crêpes to the table after the flame is extinguished.

CRÊPES SUZETTE

PREPARATION TIME 15 MINUTES (PLUS STANDING TIME) • COOKING TIME 25 MINUTES • SERVES 4

¾ cup (110g) plain flour
3 eggs
2 tablespoons vegetable oil
¾ cup (180ml) milk
ORANGE SAUCE
125g butter
½ cup (110g) caster sugar
1½ cups (375ml) orange juice, strained
2 tablespoons lemon juice
⅓ cup (80ml) orange-flavoured liqueur

1 Sift flour into medium bowl, make well in centre; add eggs and oil, gradually whisk in milk until smooth. Pour batter into large jug, cover; stand 1 hour.
2 Heat greased heavy-based crêpe pan or small frying pan; pour ¼ cup of batter into pan, tilting pan to coat base. Cook over low heat until browned lightly, loosening around edge with spatula. Turn crêpe; brown other side. Remove crêpe from pan; cover to keep warm. Repeat with remaining batter to make a total of 8 crêpes.
3 Make orange sauce.
4 Fold crêpes in half then in half again, place in sauce; warm over low heat. Divide crêpes among serving plates; pour hot sauce over crêpes. Serve with orange segments and whipped cream, if desired.
ORANGE SAUCE Melt butter in large frying pan, add sugar; cook, stirring, until mixture begins to brown. Add juices; bring to a boil. Reduce heat; simmer, uncovered, about 3 minutes or until light golden. Add liqueur; remove from heat, ignite.

IMPOSSIBLE PIE

PREPARATION TIME 10 MINUTES • COOKING TIME 45 MINUTES • SERVES 8

½ cup (75g) plain flour
1 cup (220g) caster sugar
¾ cup (60g) desiccated coconut
4 eggs
1 teaspoon vanilla extract
125g butter, melted
½ cup (40g) flaked almonds
2 cups (500ml) milk

1 Preheat oven to 180°C/160°C fan-forced. Grease deep 24cm pie dish.
2 Combine sifted flour, sugar, coconut, eggs, extract, butter and half the nuts in large bowl; gradually add milk, stirring, until combined. Pour into dish; bake 35 minutes.
3 Remove pie from oven. Sprinkle remaining nuts over pie; bake 10 minutes. Serve pie with cream or fruit, if desired.
HOW TO KEEP Store impossible pie in refrigerator, covered, for up to 2 days.

You'll discover when you make this pie how it got its name: when cooked, the pie magically separates into three perfect layers. Impossible!

LEMON DELICIOUS PUDDING

PREPARATION TIME 20 MINUTES • COOKING TIME 45 MINUTES • SERVES 6

125g butter, melted
2 teaspoons finely grated lemon rind
1½ cups (330g) caster sugar
3 eggs, separated
½ cup (75g) self-raising flour
⅓ cup (80ml) lemon juice
1⅓ cups (330ml) milk

1 Preheat oven to 180°C/160°C fan-forced. Grease six 1-cup (250ml) ovenproof dishes.

2 Combine butter, rind, sugar and yolks in large bowl. Stir in sifted flour then juice. Gradually stir in milk; mixture should be smooth and runny.

3 Beat egg whites in small bowl with electric mixer until soft peaks form; fold into lemon mixture, in two batches.

4 Place ovenproof dishes in large baking dish; divide lemon mixture among dishes. Add enough boiling water to baking dish to come halfway up sides of ovenproof dishes. Bake, uncovered, about 45 minutes.

LEMON MERINGUE PIE

½ cup (75g) cornflour
1 cup (220g) caster sugar
½ cup (125ml) lemon juice
1¼ cups (310ml) water
2 teaspoons finely grated lemon rind
60g unsalted butter, chopped
3 eggs, separated
½ cup (110g) caster sugar, extra

PASTRY
1½ cups (225g) plain flour
1 tablespoon icing sugar
140g cold butter, chopped
1 egg yolk
2 tablespoons cold water

1 Make pastry.

2 Grease 24cm-round loose-based fluted flan tin. Roll pastry between sheets of baking paper until large enough to line tin. Ease pastry into tin, press into base and side; trim edge. Cover; refrigerate 30 minutes.

3 Preheat oven to 240°C/220°C fan-forced.

4 Place tin on oven tray. Line pastry case with baking paper; fill with dried beans or rice. Bake 15 minutes; remove paper and beans carefully from pie shell. Bake about 10 minutes; cool pie shell, turn oven off.

5 Meanwhile, combine cornflour and sugar in medium saucepan; gradually stir in juice and the water until smooth. Cook, stirring, over high heat, until mixture boils and thickens. Reduce heat; simmer, stirring, 1 minute. Remove from heat; stir in rind, butter and egg yolks. Cool 10 minutes.

6 Spread filling into pie shell. Cover; refrigerate 2 hours.

7 Preheat oven to 240°C/220°C fan-forced.

8 Beat egg whites in small bowl with electric mixer until soft peaks form; gradually add extra sugar, beating until sugar dissolves.

9 Roughen surface of filling with fork before spreading with meringue mixture. Bake about 2 minutes or until browned lightly.

PASTRY Process flour, icing sugar and butter until crumbly. Add egg yolk and the water; process until ingredients come together. Knead dough on floured surface until smooth. Cover; refrigerate 30 minutes.

HOW TO KEEP Lemon meringue is best made and eaten on the same day.

Fabulous wines for every
occasion

From sparkling Prosecco to a zesty

LIME CHIFFON PIE

PREPARATION TIME 20 MINUTES (PLUS REFRIGERATION TIME) • COOKING TIME 15 MINUTES • SERVES 6

250g plain sweet biscuits
125g butter, melted
4 eggs, separated
⅓ cup (75g) caster sugar
3 teaspoons gelatine
2 teaspoons finely grated lime rind
⅓ cup (80ml) lime juice
⅓ cup (80ml) water
⅓ cup (75g) caster sugar, extra

1 Grease deep 23cm pie dish.

2 Process biscuits until fine; add butter, process until combined. Press mixture firmly over base and side of dish; refrigerate 30 minutes.

3 Combine egg yolks, sugar, gelatine, rind, juice and the water in medium heatproof bowl. Whisk over medium saucepan of simmering water until mixture thickens slightly. Remove from heat; pour into large bowl. Cover; cool.

4 Beat egg whites in small bowl with electric mixer until soft peaks form; gradually add extra sugar, beating until sugar dissolves. Fold meringue into filling mixture, in two batches.

5 Spread filling into crumb crust; refrigerate 3 hours.

TIP This recipe will make eight 8cm pies if the biscuit crumb mixture is doubled; the filling recipe above, however, is sufficient for 8 individual pies.

HOW TO KEEP Store chiffon pie in refrigerator, covered, for up to 2 days.

CHOCOLATE SELF-SAUCING PUDDING

PREPARATION TIME 20 MINUTES • COOKING TIME 45 MINUTES • SERVES 6

60g butter
½ cup (125ml) milk
½ teaspoon vanilla extract
¾ cup (165g) caster sugar
1 cup (150g) self-raising flour
1 tablespoon cocoa powder
¾ cup (165g) firmly packed
    brown sugar
1 tablespoon cocoa powder, extra
2 cups (500ml) boiling water

1 Preheat oven to 180°C/160°C fan-forced. Grease 1.5-litre (6-cup) ovenproof dish.
2 Melt butter with milk in medium saucepan. Remove from heat; stir in extract and caster sugar then sifted flour and cocoa. Spread mixture into dish.
3 Sift brown sugar and extra cocoa over mixture; gently pour boiling water over mixture. Bake about 40 minutes or until centre is firm. Stand 5 minutes before serving.

DATE AND BUTTERSCOTCH SELF-SAUCING PUDDING

PREPARATION TIME 20 MINUTES • COOKING TIME 45 MINUTES • SERVES 6

1 cup (150g) self-raising flour
½ cup (110g) firmly packed
    brown sugar
20g butter, melted
½ cup (125ml) milk
½ cup (70g) finely chopped
    dried seedless dates
CARAMEL SAUCE
½ cup (110g) firmly packed
    brown sugar
1¾ cups (430ml) boiling water
50g butter

1 Preheat oven to 180°C/160°C fan-forced. Grease 2-litre (8-cup) shallow ovenproof dish.
2 Combine flour, sugar, butter, milk and dates in medium bowl. Spread mixture into dish.
3 Make caramel sauce.
4 Pour caramel sauce slowly over back of spoon onto mixture in dish. Bake about 45 minutes or until centre is firm. Stand 5 minutes before serving.
CARAMEL SAUCE Combine ingredients in medium heatproof jug; stir until sugar is dissolved.

MOCHA, PEAR AND NUT SELF-SAUCING PUDDING

PREPARATION TIME 35 MINUTES • COOKING TIME 35 MINUTES • SERVES 8

100g dark eating chocolate, chopped
150g butter
⅔ cup (160ml) milk
1½ tablespoons instant coffee granules
⅔ cup (70g) hazelnut meal
¾ cup (165g) firmly packed
    brown sugar
1 cup (150g) self-raising flour
1 egg
2 medium pears (460g), sliced thinly
1¾ cups (430ml) water
¾ cup (165g) firmly packed
    brown sugar, extra
½ cup (50g) cocoa powder

1 Preheat oven to 180°C/160°C fan-forced. Grease eight 1¼-cup (310ml) ovenproof dishes or a shallow 2.5-litre (10-cup) ovenproof dish.
2 Stir chocolate, 50g of the butter, milk and coffee in small saucepan over low heat until smooth. Transfer to large bowl; stir in meal, sugar, then sifted flour and egg.
3 Place pear slices, slightly overlapping, in dishes; top with chocolate mixture.
4 Stir the water, extra sugar, sifted cocoa and remaining butter in small saucepan over low heat until smooth; pour over chocolate mixture. Bake about 30 minutes (or about 45 minutes for larger pudding). Stand 5 minutes before serving.

date and butterscotch self-saucing pudding

chocolate self-saucing pudding

mocha, pear and nut self-saucing pudding

HOW TO KEEP Puddings
can be stored, refrigerated, in an
airtight container for 2 days.

STEAMED GINGER PUDDING

PREPARATION TIME 15 MINUTES • COOKING TIME 1 HOUR • SERVES 6

60g butter
¼ cup (90g) golden syrup
½ teaspoon bicarbonate of soda
1 cup (150g) self-raising flour
2 teaspoons ground ginger
½ cup (125ml) milk
1 egg

SYRUP
⅓ cup (115g) golden syrup
2 tablespoons water
30g butter

1 Grease 1.25-litre (5-cup) pudding steamer.
2 Combine butter and syrup in small saucepan; stir over low heat until smooth. Remove from heat, stir in soda; transfer mixture to medium bowl. Stir in sifted dry ingredients then combined milk and egg, in two batches.
3 Spread mixture into steamer. Cover with pleated baking paper and foil; secure with lid.
4 Place pudding steamer in large saucepan with enough boiling water to come halfway up side of steamer; cover pan with tight-fitting lid. Boil 1 hour, replenishing water as necessary to maintain level. Stand pudding 5 minutes before turning onto plate.
5 Meanwhile, make syrup.
6 Serve pudding topped with syrup and, if desired, cream.
SYRUP Stir ingredients in small saucepan over heat until smooth; bring to a boil. Reduce heat; simmer, uncovered, 2 minutes.

This version of the light-as-air dessert was created in 1935 by a chef at Perth's Esplanade Hotel, and named by an employee at the same hotel because, it is said, the confection reminded him of the famous Russian ballerina's tutu.

MARSHMALLOW PAVLOVA

PREPARATION TIME 25 MINUTES (PLUS COOLING TIME) • COOKING TIME 1 HOUR 30 MINUTES • SERVES 8

4 egg whites
1 cup (220g) caster sugar
½ teaspoon vanilla extract
¾ teaspoon white vinegar
300ml thickened cream, whipped
250g strawberries, halved

1 Preheat oven to 120°C/100°C fan-forced. Line oven tray with foil; grease foil, dust with cornflour, shake away excess. Mark 18cm-circle on foil.

2 Beat egg whites in small bowl with electric mixer until soft peaks form; gradually add sugar, beating until sugar dissolves. Add extract and vinegar; beat until combined.

3 Spread meringue into circle on foil, building up at the side to 8cm in height.

4 Smooth side and top of pavlova gently. Using spatula blade, mark decorative grooves around side of pavlova; smooth top again.

5 Bake about 1½ hours. Turn off oven; cool pavlova in oven with door ajar. When pavlova is cold, cut around top edge (the crisp meringue top will fall slightly on top of the marshmallow). Serve pavlova topped with whipped cream and strawberries; dust lightly with sifted icing sugar, if desired.

HOW TO KEEP Store unfilled pavlova in an airtight container for up to 2 days.

PECAN PIE

PREPARATION TIME 25 MINUTES (PLUS REFRIGERATION TIME) • COOKING TIME 1 HOUR • SERVES 10

1 cup (120g) pecans, chopped coarsely
2 tablespoons cornflour
1 cup (220g) firmly packed
   brown sugar
60g butter, melted
2 tablespoons cream
1 teaspoon vanilla extract
3 eggs
⅓ cup (40g) pecans, extra
2 tablespoons apricot jam,
   warmed, sieved
PASTRY
1¼ cups (185g) plain flour
⅓ cup (55g) icing sugar
125g cold butter, chopped
1 egg yolk
1 teaspoon water

1 Make pastry.

2 Grease 24cm-round loose-based flan tin. Roll pastry between sheets of baking paper until large enough to line tin. Ease pastry into tin, press into base and side; trim edge. Cover; refrigerate 30 minutes.

3 Preheat oven to 180°C/160°C fan-forced.

4 Place tin on oven tray. Line pastry case with baking paper, fill with dried beans or rice. Bake 10 minutes; remove paper and beans carefully from pie shell. Bake about 5 minutes; cool.

5   Reduce oven temperature to 160°C/140°C fan-forced.

6 Combine chopped nuts and cornflour in medium bowl. Add sugar, butter, cream, extract and eggs; stir until combined. Pour mixture into shell, sprinkle with extra nuts.

7 Bake about 45 minutes. Cool; brush pie with jam.

PASTRY Process flour, icing sugar and butter until crumbly. Add egg yolk and the water; process until ingredients just come together. Knead dough on floured surface until smooth. Cover; refrigerate 30 minutes.

HOW TO KEEP Store pecan pie in refrigerator, in an airtight container, for up to 3 days.

RICE PUDDING

½ cup (100g) uncooked white
  medium-grain rice
2½ cups (625ml) milk
¼ cup (55g) caster sugar
¼ cup (40g) sultanas
½ teaspoon vanilla extract
2 teaspoons butter
½ teaspoon ground nutmeg

1 Preheat oven to 160°C/140°C fan-forced. Grease shallow 1-litre (4-cup) baking dish.

2 Wash rice under cold water; drain well. Combine rice, milk, sugar, sultanas and extract in dish; whisk lightly with fork. Dot with butter.

3 Bake, uncovered, 1 hour, whisking lightly with fork under skin occasionally. Sprinkle with nutmeg; bake 20 minutes. Serve warm or cold.

BAKED RICE CUSTARD

4 eggs
⅓ cup (75g) caster sugar
½ teaspoon vanilla extract
2 cups (500ml) milk
300ml cream
⅓ cup (50g) raisins
1½ cups cold cooked white
  medium-grain rice
1 teaspoon ground cinnamon

1 Preheat oven to 180°C/160°C fan-forced. Grease 1.5-litre (6-cup) baking dish.

2 Whisk eggs, sugar and extract in medium bowl until combined. Whisk in milk and cream; stir in raisins and rice.

3 Pour mixture into dish. Place dish in large baking dish; pour enough boiling water into baking dish to come halfway up sides of dish. Bake 30 minutes, whisking lightly with fork under skin occasionally. Sprinkle with cinnamon; bake 20 minutes. Serve warm or cold.

CREAMED RICE

1 litre (4 cups) milk
⅓ cup (75g) caster sugar
1 teaspoon vanilla extract
½ cup (100g) uncooked white
  medium-grain rice

1 Combine milk, sugar and extract in large saucepan; bring to a boil. Gradually add rice to boiling milk. Reduce heat; simmer, covered, stirring occasionally, about 50 minutes or until rice is tender and milk is almost absorbed.

2 Serve warm or cold, with fresh berries, if desired.

baked rice custard

rice pudding

creamed rice

HOW TO KEEP Rice desserts
can be stored, refrigerated, in an
airtight container for 2 days.

APRICOT AND HONEY SOUFFLÉS
PREPARATION TIME 15 MINUTES • COOKING TIME 30 MINUTES • SERVES 6

¼ cup (55g) caster sugar
4 apricots (200g)
¼ cup (60ml) water
2 tablespoons honey
4 egg whites

1 Preheat oven to 180°C/160°C fan-forced. Grease six ¾-cup (180ml) soufflé dishes; sprinkle inside of dishes with a little of the sugar, place on oven tray.

2 Place apricots in small heatproof bowl, cover with boiling water; stand 2 minutes. Drain; cool 5 minutes. Peel and seed apricots; chop flesh finely.

3 Combine apricot in small saucepan with remaining sugar, the water and honey; bring to a boil. Reduce heat; simmer, uncovered, about 10 minutes or until apricots soften to a jam-like consistency.

4 Beat egg whites in small bowl with electric mixer until soft peaks form. With motor operating, gradually add hot apricot mixture, beating until just combined.

5 Divide soufflé mixture among dishes; bake 15 minutes. Dust with icing sugar, if desired.

BAKED APPLES

PREPARATION TIME 15 MINUTES • COOKING TIME 45 MINUTES • SERVES 4

4 large Granny Smith apples (800g)
50g butter, melted
⅓ cup (75g) firmly packed brown sugar
½ cup (80g) sultanas
1 teaspoon ground cinnamon

1 Preheat oven to 160°C/140°C fan-forced.
2 Core unpeeled apples about three-quarters of the way down from stem end, making hole 4cm in diameter. Use small sharp knife to score around centre of each apple.
3 Combine remaining ingredients in small bowl. Pack sultana mixture firmly into apples; stand apples upright in small baking dish. Bake, uncovered, about 45 minutes.

VARIATIONS

MUESLI FILLING Replace sultana mixture with ⅔ cup natural muesli, 1 cup thawed, well-drained frozen blueberries, 40g melted butter and 2 tablespoons brown sugar.
BERRY FILLING BERRY FILLING Replace sultana mixture with 1½ cups thawed well-drained frozen mixed berries. Bruise 4 cardamom pods; place one cardamom pod in each apple with mixed berries.

QUEEN OF PUDDINGS

PREPARATION TIME 20 MINUTES • COOKING TIME 40 MINUTES • SERVES 6

2 cups (140g) stale breadcrumbs
1 tablespoon caster sugar
1 teaspoon vanilla extract
1 teaspoon finely grated lemon rind
2½ cups (625ml) milk
60g butter
4 eggs, separated
¼ cup (80g) raspberry jam, warmed
¾ cup (165g) caster sugar, extra

1 Preheat oven to 180°C/160°C fan-forced. Grease six ¾-cup (180ml) ovenproof dishes; stand on oven tray.
2 Combine breadcrumbs, sugar, extract and rind in large bowl. Heat milk and butter in medium saucepan until almost boiling, pour over bread mixture; stand 10 minutes. Stir in yolks.
3 Divide mixture among dishes. Bake about 30 minutes. Carefully spread top of hot puddings with jam.
4 Beat egg whites in small bowl with electric mixer until soft peaks form; gradually add extra sugar, beating until sugar dissolves. Spoon meringue over puddings; bake about 10 minutes.

Summer pudding is commonly made using stale bread; we've developed our own version with a twist, using homemade sponge cake.

SUMMER PUDDING

PREPARATION TIME 30 MINUTES (PLUS REFRIGERATION TIME) • COOKING TIME 25 MINUTES • SERVES 6

3 eggs
½ cup (110g) caster sugar
1 tablespoon cornflour
¾ cup (110g) self-raising flour
1 teaspoon butter
¼ cup (60ml) boiling water
⅓ cup (75g) caster sugar, extra
½ cup (125ml) water
2 cups (300g) frozen blackberries
3⅓ cups (500g) frozen mixed berries
¼ cup (80g) blackberry jam

1 Preheat oven to 180°C/160°C fan-forced. Grease 25cm x 30cm swiss roll pan; line base with baking paper, extending paper 5cm over long sides.

2 Beat eggs in small bowl with electric mixer until thick and creamy. Gradually add sugar, beating until sugar dissolves; transfer mixture to large bowl.

3 Fold triple-sifted flours into egg mixture. Pour combined butter and boiling water down side of bowl; fold into egg mixture. Spread mixture into pan; bake 15 minutes. Cool in pan.

4 Meanwhile, combine extra sugar and the water in medium saucepan; bring to a boil. Stir in berries; return to a boil. Reduce heat; simmer, uncovered, until berries soften. Strain over medium bowl; reserve syrup and berries separately.

5 Turn cake onto board. Line 1.25-litre (5-cup) pudding basin with plastic wrap, extending wrap 10cm over side of basin. Cut circle slightly smaller than top edge of basin from cake using tip of sharp knife; cut second circle exact size of base of basin from cake. Cut remaining cake into 10cm long strips.

6 Place small cake circle in base of basin and use cake strips to line side of basin. Pour ⅔ cup of the reserved syrup into small jug; reserve. Fill basin with berries; cover with remaining syrup, top with large cake circle. Cover pudding with overhanging plastic wrap, weight pudding with saucer; refrigerate 3 hours or overnight.

7 Stir jam and two tablespoons of the reserved syrup in small saucepan until heated through. Turn pudding onto serving plate; brush with remaining reserved syrup then jam mixture. Serve with whipped cream, if desired.

VANILLA BEAN ICE-CREAM

PREPARATION TIME 15 MINUTES (PLUS REFRIGERATION, CHURNING AND FREEZING TIME)
COOKING TIME 10 MINUTES • SERVES 8

----

2 vanilla beans
1⅔ cups (410ml) milk
600ml thickened cream
8 egg yolks
¾ cup (165g) caster sugar

1 Split vanilla beans lengthways; scrape out seeds into medium saucepan. Add pods, milk and cream; bring to a boil.

2 Meanwhile, whisk egg yolks and sugar in medium bowl until creamy; gradually whisk into hot milk mixture. Stir over low heat, without boiling, until mixture thickens slightly.

3 Strain mixture into medium heatproof bowl; discard pods. Cover surface of custard with plastic wrap; refrigerate about 1 hour or until cold.

4 Pour custard into ice-cream maker, churn according to manufacturer's instructions (or place custard in shallow container, such as an aluminium slab cake pan, cover with foil; freeze until almost firm). Place ice-cream in large bowl, chop coarsely then beat with electric mixer until smooth. Pour into deep container, cover; freeze until firm. Repeat process two more times.

HOW TO KEEP Store ice-cream in freezer, covered, for up to 4 weeks.

VARIATIONS

PASSIONFRUIT Omit vanilla beans; reduce milk to 1 cup. Stir ⅔ cup passionfruit pulp into custard before placing in ice-cream maker.

CHOCOLATE Omit vanilla beans; add 20g coarsely chopped dark eating chocolate to milk and cream when heating.

CLASSIC TRIFLE

PREPARATION TIME 30 MINUTES (PLUS REFRIGERATION TIME) • COOKING TIME 10 MINUTES • SERVES 8

85g packet raspberry jelly crystals
250g sponge cake, cut into 3cm pieces
¼ cup (60ml) sweet sherry
¼ cup (30g) custard powder
¼ cup (55g) caster sugar
½ teaspoon vanilla extract
1½ cups (375ml) milk
825g can sliced peaches, drained
300ml thickened cream
2 tablespoons flaked almonds, roasted

1 Make jelly according to directions on packet; pour into shallow container. Refrigerate 20 minutes or until jelly is almost set.
2 Arrange cake in 3-litre (12-cup) bowl; sprinkle with sherry.
3 Blend custard powder, sugar and extract with a little of the milk in small saucepan; stir in remaining milk. Stir over heat until mixture boils and thickens. Cover surface with plastic wrap; cool.
4 Pour jelly over cake; refrigerate 15 minutes. Top with peaches. Stir a third of the cream into custard; pour over peaches.
5 Whip remaining cream; spread over custard, sprinkle with nuts. Refrigerate 3 hours or overnight.

CHOCOLATE AND BERRY TRIFLE

PREPARATION TIME 30 MINUTES (PLUS REFRIGERATION TIME) • COOKING TIME 10 MINUTES • SERVES 6

150g dark eating chocolate, chopped coarsely
¾ cup (180ml) thickened cream
1 egg, separated
2 teaspoons caster sugar
85g packet cherry jelly crystals
325g un-iced chocolate cake, chopped coarsely
300g fresh mixed berries

1 Stir chocolate and cream in small saucepan over low heat until smooth. Remove from heat; transfer to medium bowl; stir in egg yolk.
2 Beat egg white and sugar in small bowl with electric mixer until sugar dissolves; fold into chocolate mixture. Refrigerate mousse 3 hours or overnight.
3 Make jelly according to directions on packet; pour into shallow container. Refrigerate 20 minutes or until jelly is almost set.
4 Place cake pieces in six 1-cup (250ml) serving glasses.
5 Pour jelly over cake; refrigerate 15 minutes. Divide half the berries over the jelly; top with scoops of mousse, then remaining berries.

TROPICAL FRUIT TRIFLE

PREPARATION TIME 25 MINUTES (PLUS REFRIGERATION TIME) • COOKING TIME 5 MINUTES • SERVES 6

85g packet mango jelly crystals
¼ cup (30g) custard powder
⅓ cup (75g) caster sugar
½ teaspoon vanilla extract
1½ cups (375ml) milk
⅓ cup (80ml) pineapple juice
⅓ cup (80ml) coconut-flavoured liqueur
6 savoiardi sponge fingers
⅔ cup (160ml) thickened cream
125g cream cheese, softened
1 medium kiwi fruit (85g), sliced
1 medium mango (430g), sliced
1 medium star fruit (160g), sliced
2 tablespoons passionfruit pulp

1 Make jelly according to directions on packet; pour into shallow container. Refrigerate 20 minutes or until jelly is almost set.
2 Blend custard powder, half the sugar, and extract with a little of the milk in small saucepan; stir in remaining milk. Stir over heat until mixture boils and thickens. Cover custard surface with plastic wrap; cool.
3 Combine juice and liqueur in small bowl. Soak sponge fingers, one at a time, in juice mixture; place over base of shallow 2-litre (8-cup) serving dish. Pour jelly over sponge fingers, cover; refrigerate 15 minutes or until jelly is set.
4 Stir half the cream into custard; pour over jelly.
5 Beat cream cheese with remaining cream and sugar in small bowl with electric mixer until smooth. Spread over custard, top with fruit and pulp. Refrigerate 3 hours or overnight.

classic trifle

chocolate and berry trifle

tropical fruit trifle

HOW TO KEEP Trifles can be
stored, refrigerated, overnight.

CRÈME CARAMEL

PREPARATION TIME 20 MINUTES (PLUS REFRIGERATION TIME) • COOKING TIME 40 MINUTES • SERVES 6

¾ cup (165g) caster sugar
½ cup (125ml) water
300ml cream
1¾ cups (430ml) milk
6 eggs
1 teaspoon vanilla extract
⅓ cup (75g) caster sugar, extra

1 Preheat oven to 160°C/140°C fan-forced.
2 Combine sugar and the water in medium frying pan; stir over heat, without boiling, until sugar dissolves. Bring to a boil; boil, uncovered, without stirring, until mixture is deep caramel in colour. Remove from heat; allow bubbles to subside. Pour toffee into deep 20cm-round cake pan.
3 Combine cream and milk in medium saucepan; bring to a boil. Whisk eggs, extract and extra sugar in large bowl; whisking constantly, pour hot milk mixture into egg mixture. Strain mixture into cake pan.
4 Place pan in medium baking dish; add enough boiling water to come half way up side of pan. Bake, uncovered, about 40 minutes or until firm. Remove custard from baking dish, cover; refrigerate overnight.
5 Gently ease crème caramel from side of pan; invert onto deep-sided serving plate.

VARIATIONS

VANILLA BEAN Add 1 split vanilla bean to cream and milk mixture before bringing to a boil; strain, remove vanilla bean before adding to egg mixture.
CINNAMON Add 1 cinnamon stick to cream and milk mixture before bringing to a boil; strain, remove cinnamon stick before adding to egg mixture.
ORANGE Stir 2 teaspoons finely grated orange rind into custard mixture before baking.
HAZELNUT Add 1 cup coarsely chopped roasted hazelnuts to cream and milk mixture; bring to a boil. Cover; stand 20 minutes then strain through muslin-lined sieve. Discard nuts. Bring cream and milk mixture back to a boil before whisking into egg mixture.

CRÈME BRÛLÉE

PREPARATION TIME 15 MINUTES (PLUS REFRIGERATION TIME) • COOKING TIME 40 MINUTES • SERVES 6

1 vanilla bean
3 cups (750ml) thickened cream
6 egg yolks
¼ cup (55g) caster sugar
¼ cup (40g) pure icing sugar

1 Preheat oven to 180°C/160°C fan-forced. Grease six ½-cup (125ml) ovenproof dishes.

2 Split vanilla bean in half lengthways; scrape seeds into medium heatproof bowl. Heat pod with cream in small saucepan, without boiling.

3 Add egg yolks and caster sugar to seeds in bowl; gradually whisk in hot cream mixture. Set bowl over medium saucepan of simmering water; stir over heat about 10 minutes or until custard mixture thickens slightly and coats the back of a spoon; discard pod.

4 Place dishes in large baking dish; divide custard among dishes. Add enough boiling water to baking dish to come halfway up sides of ovenproof dishes. Bake, uncovered, in oven about 20 minutes or until custard sets. Remove custards from dish; cool. Cover; refrigerate overnight.

5 Preheat grill. Place custards in shallow flameproof dish filled with ice cubes; sprinkle custards evenly with sifted icing sugar. Using finger, spread sugar over the surface of each custard, pressing in gently; grill until tops of crème brûlée caramelise.

VARIATION

SUGAR-CRUSTED Replace icing sugar with ¼ cup caster sugar, 2 tablespoons brown sugar and 2 tablespoons grated palm sugar.

GLOSSARY

ALMOND
blanched brown skins removed.
essence synthetically produced from flavouring, oil and alcohol.
flaked paper-thin slices.
meal also known as ground almonds; nuts are powdered to a flour-like texture. For use in baking or as a thickening agent.
slivered small pieces cut lengthways.

ARROWROOT a starch made from the root of a Central American plant, used mostly as a thickening agent. Cornflour can be substituted, but does not make as clear a glaze and imparts its own taste.

BICARBONATE OF SODA a raising agent also known as baking soda.

BISCUITS also known as cookies; almost always a hand-sized soft or crisp sweet cake.

BRANDY short for brandywine, the translation of the Dutch "brandwijn", burnt wine. A general term for a liqueur distilled from wine grapes (usually white), it is used as the basis for many sweet-to-dry spirits made with fruits. Cognac and Armagnac are two of the finest aged brandies.

BREADCRUMBS, STALE crumbs made by grating, blending or processing 1- or 2-day-old bread.

BRIOCHE French in origin; a rich, yeast-leavened, cake-like bread made with butter and eggs. Most common form is the brioche à tête, a round fluted roll topped with a much smaller ball of dough. Available from cake or specialty bread shops.

BUTTER use salted or unsalted ("sweet") butter; 125g is equal to one stick of butter.

BUTTERMILK originally the term given to the slightly sour liquid left after butter was churned from cream, today it is commercially made similarly to yogurt. Sold alongside fresh milk products in supermarkets.

CALROSE RICE a white medium-grain rice that can be substituted for short- or long-grain varieties.

CHERRY-FLAVOURED BRANDY you can use Kirsch or any other cherry-flavoured brandy.

CHOCOLATE
Choc Bits also known as chocolate chips and chocolate morsels; available in milk, white and dark chocolate. Made of cocoa liquor, cocoa butter, sugar and an emulsifier, these hold their shape in baking and are ideal for decorating.
chocolate Melts small discs of compounded milk, white or dark chocolate ideal for melting and moulding into shapes.
dark eating made of cocoa liquor, cocoa butter and sugar.
milk eating most popular eating chocolate, mild and very sweet; similar in make-up to dark with the difference being the addition of milk solids.
white eating contains no cocoa solids but derives its sweet flavour from cocoa butter. Very sensitive to heat.
chocolate hazelnut spread you can use Nutella or any other chocolate hazelnut spread.

CIABATTA in Italian, the word means slipper, the traditional shape of this popular crisp-crusted, open-textured white sourdough bread.

CINNAMON dried inner bark of the shoots of the cinnamon tree; available in stick or ground form.
sugar combination of ground cinnamon and caster sugar.

COCOA POWDER also known as cocoa; cocoa beans (cacao seeds) that have been fermented, roasted, shelled, ground into powder then cleared of most of the fat content.

COCONUT
coconut-flavoured rum you can use Malibu or any other coconut-flavoured rum.
desiccated concentrated, dried, unsweetened and finely shredded coconut flesh.
essence synthetically produced from flavouring, oil and alcohol.

COFFEE-FLAVOURED LIQUEUR an alcoholic syrup distilled from wine or brandy and flavoured with coffee. Use Tia Maria, Kahlua or any other coffee-flavoured liqueur.

CORNFLAKES commercially manufactured cereal made of dehydrated then baked crisp flakes of corn. Also available is a prepared finely ground mixture used for coating or crumbing food before frying or baking; sold as "crushed corn flakes" in 300g packages in most supermarkets.

CORNFLOUR also known as cornstarch; used as a thickening agent in cooking.
wheaten cornflour made with wheat as opposed to corn; available from all supermarkets.

CRAISINS dried cranberries; packaged like raisins and sultanas and available in supermarkets. Can usually be substituted for or with other dried fruit in most recipes.

CREAM
crème fraîche mature fermented cream having a slightly tangy, nutty flavour and velvety texture. Used in both savoury and sweet dishes.
sour thick, commercially-cultured soured cream.
thickened a whipping cream that contains a thickener.

CREAM CHEESE commonly known as Philadelphia or Philly; a soft cow-milk cheese. Sold at supermarkets in bulk and packaged.

CREAM OF TARTAR the acid ingredient in baking powder; added to confectionery mixtures to help prevent sugar crystallising. Keeps frostings creamy and improves volume when beating egg whites.

DATES fruits of the date palm tree, thought to have originated in North Africa, which have a thick, sticky texture and sweet mild flavour. Sometimes sold already pitted and chopped; can be eaten fresh or dried on their own, or cooked to release their flavour.

FLOUR
plain an all-purpose flour made from wheat.
rice a very fine flour made from ground white rice.
self-raising all-purpose plain or wholemeal flour sifted with baking powder in the proportion of 1 cup flour to 2 teaspoons baking powder.

FRUIT MINCE a mixture of dried fruits, peel, rind, sugar, alcohol and spices. When cooked, the mixture forms a rich, fruity spread; commonly used as a filling in fruit mince pies.

GELATINE we use dried (powdered) gelatine in the recipes in this book; it's also available in sheet form known as leaf gelatine. Three teaspoons of dried gelatine (8g or one sachet) is roughly equivalent to four gelatine leaves. The two types are interchangable, but leaf gelatine gives a much clearer mixture than dried gelatine; it's perfect in dishes where appearance really counts.

GINGER
crystallised fresh ginger, cubed and preserved in syrup and then coated in sugar.
glacé fresh ginger root preserved in sugar syrup. Crystallised ginger can be substituted if rinsed with warm water and dried before using.
ground also known as powdered ginger; used as a flavouring in cakes, pies and puddings, but cannot be substituted for fresh ginger.

GLACE CHERRIES cherries cooked in a heavy sugar syrup then dried.

GOLDEN SYRUP a by-product of refined sugarcane; pure maple syrup or honey can be substituted.

HAZELNUTS also known as filberts; plump, grape-sized, rich, sweet nut having a brown inedible skin that is removed by rubbing heated nuts together vigorously in a tea towel.
meal also known as ground hazelnut.
spread a chocolate hazelnut spread available from supermarkets.

LAMINGTON PAN 20cm x 30cm slab cake pan, 3cm deep.

MACADAMIA native to Australia, a rich and buttery nut; store in the refrigerator because of its high oil content.

MAPLE SYRUP a thin syrup distilled from the sap of the maple tree. Maple-flavoured syrup or pancake syrup is not an adequate substitute.

MIXED PEEL candied citrus peel.

MIXED SPICE a classic mixture generally containing caraway, allspice, coriander, cumin, nutmeg and ginger, although cinnamon and other spices can be added.

NUTMEG a strong and very pungent spice ground from the dried nut of an evergreen tree native to Indonesia. Usually found ground, but the flavour is more intense from a whole nut, available from spice shops, so it's best to grate your own.

OIL, VEGETABLE any of a number of oils sourced from plant rather than animal fats.

ORANGE-FLAVOURED LIQUEUR use Cointreau, Grand Marnier, Curaçao or any other orange-flavoured liqueur.

PASTRY
fillo also known as phyllo pastry; tissue-thin pastry sheets purchased chilled or frozen.
ready-rolled puff packaged sheets of frozen puff pastry, available from major supermarkets.

PECAN native to the United States and now grown locally; golden-brown, buttery and rich in flavour.

PINE NUT also known as pignoli; not, in fact, a nut but a small, cream-coloured kernel from pine cones.

ROLLED OATS flattened oat grain rolled into flakes and traditionally used for porridge. Instant oats are also available, but use traditional oats for baking.

SAVOIARDI SPONGE FINGERS also known as savoy biscuits, lady's fingers or sponge fingers, they are Italian-style crisp fingers made from sponge-cake mixture.

STAR FRUIT also known as carambola, five-corner fruit or chinese star fruit; pale green or yellow in colour, it has a clean, crisp texture. Flavour may be either sweet or sour, depending on the variety and when it was picked. There is no need to peel or seed it and they're slow to discolour.

SUGAR
brown a soft, finely granulated sugar containing molasses, which gives it its characteristic colour and flavour.
caster also known as superfine or finely granulated table sugar.
demerara sugar small-grained, golden-coloured crystal sugar.
icing sugar also known as confectioners' sugar or powdered sugar; granulated sugar crushed with a small amount of cornflour.
palm also known as jaggery, nam tan pip, jawa or gula melaka; made from the sap of the sugar palm tree. Light brown to black in colour and usually sold in rock-hard cakes; if unavailable, substitute palm sugar with brown sugar.
white also known as granulated or crystal sugar.

SULTANAS also known as golden raisins; dried seedless white grapes.

SWEET SHERRY a fortified wine.

SWEETENED CONDENSED MILK a canned milk product consisting of milk with more than half the water content removed and sugar added to the milk that remains.

VANILLA
bean dried, long, thin pod from a tropical golden orchid; the minuscule black seeds inside the bean are used to impart a luscious vanilla flavour in baking and desserts. A bean can be used three or four times before losing its flavour.
bean paste made from vanilla bean extract, vanilla bean seeds, sugar and natural thickeners. Can be used as a substitute for vanilla bean.
extract vanilla beans that have been submerged in alcohol. Vanilla essence is not a suitable substitute.

CONVERSION CHART

MEASURES

One Australian metric measuring cup holds approximately 250ml; one Australian metric tablespoon holds 20ml; one Australian metric teaspoon holds 5ml.

The difference between one country's measuring cups and another's is within a two- or three-teaspoon variance, and will not affect your cooking results. North America, New Zealand and the United Kingdom use a 15ml tablespoon.

All cup and spoon measurements are level. The most accurate way of measuring dry ingredients is to weigh them. When measuring liquids, use a clear glass or plastic jug with the metric markings.

We use large eggs with an average weight of 60g.

DRY MEASURES

METRIC	IMPERIAL
15g	½oz
30g	1oz
60g	2oz
90g	3oz
125g	4oz (¼lb)
155g	5oz
185g	6oz
220g	7oz
250g	8oz (½lb)
280g	9oz
315g	10oz
345g	11oz
375g	12oz (¾lb)
410g	13oz
440g	14oz
470g	15oz
500g	16oz (1lb)
750g	24oz (1½lb)
1kg	32oz (2lb)

LIQUID MEASURES

METRIC	IMPERIAL
30ml	1 fluid oz
60ml	2 fluid oz
100ml	3 fluid oz
125ml	4 fluid oz
150ml	5 fluid oz (¼ pint/1 gill)
190ml	6 fluid oz
250ml	8 fluid oz
300ml	10 fluid oz (½ pint)
500ml	16 fluid oz
600ml	20 fluid oz (1 pint)
1000ml (1 litre)	1¾ pints

LENGTH MEASURES

METRIC	IMPERIAL
3mm	⅛in
6mm	¼in
1cm	½in
2cm	¾in
2.5cm	1in
5cm	2in
6cm	2½in
8cm	3in
10cm	4in
13cm	5in
15cm	6in
18cm	7in
20cm	8in
23cm	9in
25cm	10in
28cm	11in
30cm	12in (1ft)

OVEN TEMPERATURES

These oven temperatures are only a guide for conventional ovens. For fan-forced ovens, check the manufacturer's manual.

	°C (CELSIUS)	°F (FAHRENHEIT)	GAS MARK
Very slow	120	250	½
Slow	150	275-300	1-2
Moderately slow	160	325	3
Moderate	180	350-375	4-5
Moderately hot	200	400	6
Hot	220	425-450	7-8
Very hot	240	475	9

INDEX

If you like this cookbook, you'll love these...

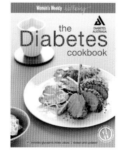

TEST KITCHEN
Food director Pamela Clark
Assistant food editor Sarah Schwikkard
Home economists Belinda Farlow, Miranda Farr,
Nicole Jennings, Elizabeth Macri, Kirrily La Rosa,
Rebecca Squadrito, Kellie-Marie Thomas, Mary Wills

ACP BOOKS
General manager Christine Whiston
Editorial director Susan Tomnay
Creative director & designer Hieu Chi Nguyen
Senior editor Wendy Bryant
Director of sales Brian Cearnes
Marketing manager Bridget Cody
Business analyst Rebecca Varela
Operations manager David Scotto
Production manager Victoria Jefferys
International rights enquiries Laura Bamford
lbamford@acpuk.com

ACP Books are published by ACP Magazines
a division of PBL Media Pty Limited
Group publisher, Women's lifestyle Pat Ingram
Director of sales, Women's lifestyle Lynette Phillips
Commercial manager, Women's lifestyle Seymour Cohen
Marketing director, Women's lifestyle Matthew Dominello
Public relations manager, Women's lifestyle Hannah Deveraux
Creative director, Events, Women's lifestyle Luke Bonnano
Research Director, Women's lifestyle Justin Stone
ACP Magazines, Chief Executive officer Scott Lorson
PBL Media, Chief Executive officer Ian Law

Produced by ACP Books, Sydney.
Published by ACP Books, a division of ACP Magazines Ltd,
54 Park St, Sydney; GPO Box 4088, Sydney, NSW 2001.
phone (02) 9282 8618 fax (02) 9267 9438.
acpbooks@acpmagazines.com.au
www.acpbooks.com.au
Printed by Dai Nippon in Korea.

Australia Distributed by Network Services,
phone +61 2 9282 8777 fax +61 2 9264 3278
networkweb@networkservicescompany.com.au
United Kingdom Distributed by Australian Consolidated Press (UK),
phone (01604) 642 200 fax (01604) 642 300
books@acpuk.com
New Zealand Distributed by Netlink Distribution Company,
phone (9) 366 9966 ask@ndc.co.nz
South Africa Distributed by PSD Promotions,
phone (27 11) 392 6065/6/7 fax (27 11) 392 6079/80
orders@psdprom.co.za
Canada Distributed by Publishers Group Canada
phone (800) 663 5714 fax (800) 565 3770
service@raincoast.com

The Australian Women's Weekly Pamela Clark.
Old-fashioned favourites.
Includes index.
ISBN 978-1-86396577-4
1. Baking. 2. Desserts. 3. Cake. 4. Biscuits.
I. Clark, Pamela.
641.86
© ACP Magazines Ltd 2007
ABN 18 053 273 546

This publication is copyright. No part of it may be reproduced or
transmitted in any form without the written permission of the publishers.
First published 2007. Reprinted 2008.

The publishers would like to thank the following for props
used in photography: All Handmade Gallery; Papaya; Tres Fabu.
To order books,
phone 136 116 (within Australia).
Send recipe enquiries to:
askpamela@acpmagazines.com.au